Chapter 1: Blockchain Basics

1. Who invented blockchain?

   A. Leaonhar Euler
   B. Issae Newton
   C. Amedeo Avogrado
   D. Satoshi Nakamoto

2. What is blockchain?

   A. It is a centralized network
   B. It is a concept
   C. It is cryptographic process
   D. It is decentralized ledger distributed over p2p network

3. Which of the following best defines the decentralized ledger tracking digital assets on the p2p network?

   A. Bitcoin
   B. Blockchain
   C. Ethereum
   D. None of them

4. In which of the following network, controls are distributed among few nodes?

   A. Centralized network
   B. Distributed network
   C. Decentralized network
   D. All of them

5. In which of the following network, controls are distributed among all the nodes?

   A. Centralized network
   B. Distributed network
   C. Decentralized network
   D. All of them

6. What is bitcoin? Choose the best

   A. Virtual currency
   B. Cryptocurrency
   C. Digital currency
   D. None of the above

7. The transactions associated to the bitcoin's address are stored on?

   A. Bitcoin
   B. Ethereum
   C. Block
   D. Ripple

8. Which consensus algorithm is used in bitcoin platform?

   A. Proof of state
   B. Proof of work
   C. RPCA
   D. None of them

9. Bitcoin is equal to?

   A. Unicorn
   B. Toy silver unicorn

C. Toy golden unicorn

D. All of the above

10. Which about the following statement is used to define the computer program code that is capable of the facility, executing and enforcing the negotiation or the performance of an agreement by using blockchain technology?

    A. Proof of work

    B. Smart contract

    C. Cryptocurrency

    D. Proof of state

11. What are the benefits by using blockchain technology?

    A. High security

    B. High availability

    C. Verifiability and auditability

    D. Trustless

12. NEO was launched in?

    A. January 2009

    B. July 2015

    C. February 2014

    D. July 2014

13. How many functions of blockchain database? and name them.

    A. 2

    B. 3

    C. 4

D. 5

14. How many functions of the traditional database? And name them.

   A. 3
   B. 4
   C. 5
   D. 6

15. The process of recording the pending transaction by adding a new block into the blockchain through mathematical puzzle is called?

   A. Blockchain transactions
   B. Blockchain mining
   C. Double Spending
   D. None of them

16. Who is a miner?

   A. Miner validates new transactions and records them into a global ledger.
   B. Miners solves complex mathematical puzzles and get rewarded.
   C. Miners creates new blocks in the blockchain
   D. All of above
   E. None of above

17. What are the applications of blockchain?

   A. Bitcoin
   B. Ethereum
   C. NEO
   D. All of the above

18. What are the types of blockchain developer? And name them.

    A. Two
    B. Three
    C. Four
    D. Five

19. ICO stand for?

    A. Initial coin offering
    B. Internal coin offering
    C. Initial coin order
    D. None of them

20. How many kinds of ethereum applications? Name them.

    A. Two
    B. Three
    C. Four
    D. Five

21. Which is designed to find the rates between two digital assets and making it trade crypto is called?

    A. Stellar's SDEX Exchange
    B. NEO'S NEX Exchange
    C. EtherDelta
    D. None of them

22. Bitcoin was launched in?

    A. January 2009
    B. July 2015
    C. February 2014
    D. July 2014

23. Ethereum was launched in?

    E. January 2009
    F. July 2015
    G. February 2014
    H. July 2014

Chapter 2: Blockchain Intermediate

1. Asymmetric encryption uses:

   A. Proof of Stake
   B. Public and Private keys
   C. Public keys only
   D. Private keys only

2. What is a private key?

   A. A key that opens a secret door
   B. A key on your keychain
   C. A key does not give to the public
   D. A key gives to the public

3. What incentivizes the miners to give true validation of transactions?

   A. More memory
   B. A nonce
   C. Thumbs up from the community
   D. A block reward

4. What is the purpose of a nonce?

   A. Sends information to the Blockchain network
   B. A hash function
   C. Follows nouns
   D. Prevents double spending

5. What is a DAPP?

   A. A Decentralized Application
   B. A type of Cryptocurrency
   C. A condiment
   D. A type of Blockchain

6. Which is NOT a form of asymmetric encryption?

   A. Mining
   B. Passphrase
   C. Private Key
   D. Public key

7. What are the different types of tokens?

   A. Platform
   B. Privacy
   C. Currency
   D. All of the above

8. Where is the LEAST SAFE place to retain your Cryptocurrency?

   A. In your pocket
   B. At your work desk
   C. On an exchange
   D. On a hot wallet

9. Who created Bitcoin?

   A. Samsung
   B. John Mcafee
   C. Satoshi Nakamoto
   D. China

10. What does P2P stand?

   A. Product to Product
   B. Private Key to Public Key
   C. Password to Password
   D. Peer to Peer

11. What is a node?

   A. A Blockchain
   B. A computer on a Blockchain network
   C. A type of cryptocurrency
   D. An exchange

12. Where do you store your cryptocurrency?

   A. Wallet
   B. In your pocket
   C. Bank account
   D. Floppy Disk

13. What is a miner?

   A. A person performs calculations to verify a transaction
   B. Computers that validate and process Blockchain transactions
   C. A form of a blockchain
   D. An algorithm that expects the next part of the chain

14. Where can you buy a cryptocurrency?

    A. A Bitcoin ATM
    B. All of the above
    C. A private transaction
    D. An exchange

15. What is a blockchain?

    A. An exchange
    B. A centralized ledger
    C. A peer to peer network on a distributed ledger
    D. A form of Cryptocurrency

16. Which is the term for when a Blockchain splits?

    A. A fork
    B. A division
    C. A merger
    D. A sidechain

17. What is cold storage?

    A. The Internet has connected to the private key
    B. The Internet has not connected to the private key
    C. A place to hang your coat
    D. A paper wallet

18. What is a genesis block?

    A. The first block after each block having
    B. The 2nd transaction of a blockchain
    C. The first block of a blockchain
    D. A well-known block that hardcoded a hash of the Book of Genesis onto the blockchain

19. What powers the Ethereum Virtual Machine?

    A. Bitcoin
    B. Block Rewards
    C. Gas
    D. Ether

20. What is Proof of Stake?

    A. How private keys has made
    B. A transaction and block verification protocol
    C. A certificate needed to use the Blockchain
    D. A password needed to access an exchange

21. What is Nonce?

    A. Value in each block filled by Miner
    B. Hash of the block
    C. Hash of the transaction
    D. Private key

Chapter 3: Blockchain Advanced

1. Which of the following is a permission blockchain?
   A. Public
   B. Private
   C. Consortium
   D. None of the above

2. Which of the following is a permission less blockchain?
   A. Public
   B. Private
   C. Consortium
   D. None of the above

3. In private blockchain, authorize nodes can _____ the ledger information.
   A. Read
   B. Write
   C. Read & write
   D. All of the above

4. While setup your own blockchain, what is the most important thing to own?
   A. Ledger
   B. Nonce
   C. Miners
   D. Hashes

5. Which of the following platform can use to setup our own Blockchain?
   A. OpenChain
   B. Multichain
   C. Ethereum
   D. Hyperledger Fabric
   E. All of the above

6. Which blockchain platform founded by Mr. Gideon Greenspan.
   A. OpenChain
   B. Multichain
   C. Ethereum
   D. Hyperledger Fabric

7. Which blockchain platform doesn't have the concept of mining & cryptocurrency.
   A. OpenChain
   B. Multichain
   C. Ethereum
   D. Hyperledger Fabric

8. Which project hosted by Linux foundation umbrella?
   A. Hyperledger
   B. OpenChain
   C. Multichain
   D. Ethereum

9. Blockchain technology is not use in following situation.
   A. Data Immutability
   B. Store Large Data
   C. Share Common Database
   D. System Transparency

10. Blockchain technology is the most suitable for?
    A. Frequently changing rules of transaction
    B. Extraction of data from outsource
    C. Share Common Database
    D. Store Large Data

11. Which step is the beginning to setup our own blockchain?
    A. Specify the most favorable Consensus Method
    B. Defining the Goal
    C. Designing the Architecture
    D. Integrate Upcoming Technology

12. Which one of them is an optional part but enhances the features of your own blockchain?
    A. Building APIs
    B. Defining the Goal
    C. Admin- user Interface
    D. Integrate Upcoming Technology

13. Which is not the consideration of Building APIs?
    A. Generating key pairs and addresses
    B. Performing audit related functions
    C. Designing the Admin-User Interface
    D. Data storage and retrieval

14. Each blockchain contains which of the following?
    A. A hash pointer to the previous block
    B. Timestamp
    C. List of transactions
    D. All of the above

15. How many parent nodes present in a Decentralized network?
    A. One
    B. More than one
    C. No parent node
    D. Only child node

16. In P2P network, all nodes are designed in such a way that
    A. All nodes are connected to each other
    B. Each node can communicate with each other
    C. If one node fails, the other will work
    D. All of the above

17. The working of blockchain begins with
    A. Creating a new block
    B. Adding a new block
    C. Anyone requested for transaction
    D. Verification & validation of new block

18. In which of the following step consensus mechanism applied?
    A. Creating a new block
    B. Adding a new block
    C. Validation & Verification
    D. Requested for transaction

19. After validation & verification of transaction which process occurs?
    A. Creating a new block
    B. Adding a new block
    C. Transaction is completed
    D. Requested for transaction

20. Created block with verified data cannot be _____.
    A. Stored
    B. Modified
    C. Read
    D. Write

21. The architectural working of Blockchain ends with?
    A. Creating a new block
    B. Adding a new block
    C. Transaction is completed
    D. Requested for transaction

22. Smart contract works on the principle of
    A. Smart developer
    B. Smart user
    C. Smart coding
    D. Smart transaction

23. Which platform is the most suitable for Smart contract?
    A. Hyperledger
    B. OpenChain
    C. Multichain
    D. Ethereum

24. In working of smart contract, triggering an event occurs by?
    A. Nodes
    B. Coding
    C. Distributed ledger
    D. Transaction

25. In blockchain, each blockchain is linked with _____.
    A. Previous Block
    B. Next Block
    C. Not linked
    D. None of the above

Chapter 4: Blockchain Use-Cases

1. What is the fundamental principal of blockchain technology?
   A. It is a decentralized distributed database of immutable records.
   B. It is a centralized distributed database of immutable records.

2. Who is the founder of Bitcoin?
   A. Vitalik Buterin
   B. Satoshi Nakamoto

3. Who is the founder of Ethereum?
   A. Vitalik Buterin
   B. Satoshi Nakamoto

4. Which algorithm is used in Bitcoin for creating bitcoin address?
   A. AES
   B. SHA-128
   C. SHA-256
   D. RSA

5. What are the two types of record in blockchain database?
   A. Block record
   B. Miner record
   C. Transactional record
   D. Consensus record

6. Each block consists of?
   A. Time Stamp
   B. Hash Pointer
   C. Transactions
   D. All of the above
   E. None of the above

7. A block in blockchain support _____ parent block(s).
   A. 1
   B. 2
   C. 3
   D. 4

8. Which of the following are consensus algorithms?
   A. PBFT (Practical Byzantine Fault Tolerance)
   B. Proof-of-Work
   C. Proof-of-Stake
   D. Delegated Proof-of-Stake
   E. Proof-of-Elapsed time
   F. All of the above

9. How many types of blockchain are there?
   A. 1
   B. 2
   C. 3
   D. 4

10. Which type of record can a blockchain can store?
    A. Health record
    B. Business transactions
    C. Management records
    D. Financial records
    E. All of the above
    F. None of the above

11. A set of protocols which validates, exchange shares, money, or enforce the negotiation without a centralized organization is called?
    A. Smart Contracts
    B. Minting
    C. Distributed Ledger
    D. Token

12. Which technology is use to digitize a real estate transaction?
    A. Traditional technology
    B. Blockchain advance technology

13. How many copies of the contract, a system sent?
    A. 2
    B. 3
    C. 4
    D. 5

14. Which entities save the copy of the contract of sold land?
    A. Purchaser, Seller, Bank
    B. Purchaser, Seller, System
    C. Purchaser, Seller, Seller Bank
    D. Purchaser, Seller, Agent

15. How many e-paper has signed when land is sold?
    A. 3
    B. 4
    C. 5
    D. 6

16. Which master key is used in Digital Identity?
    A. Private master key
    B. Public master key

17. How much percentage can reduce the blockchain while using a cross-border payment method?
    A. 1-2%
    B. 2-3%
    C. 3-4%
    D. 4-5%

18. Which type of customer can attract to a customer loyalty program?
    A. Old customer
    B. Exciting customer
    C. New Customer

19. Which algorithm is used in Bitcoin for mining?
    A. AES
    B. SHA-128
    C. SHA-256
    D. RSA

20. How does a block is recognized in the Blockchain?
    A. Nonce
    B. Hash Pointer
    C. Hash
    D. Block ID

21. What is Double Spending?
    A. Spending a digital token multiple times
    B. Fake transactions
    C. Multiple transactions

22. Name the common type of ledgers in blockchain network?
    A. Centralized Ledgers
    B. Decentralized Ledgers
    C. Distributed Ledgers
    D. All of the above

23. Which of the following is the application of Blockchain platform "*Ripple*"?
    A. Digital Currency
    B. Cross-border payments
    C. Logistics
    D. Voting

24. Which of the following Consensus algorithm is used in "*NEO*"?
    A. Proof-of-Work
    B. Delegated Byzantine Fault Tolerance (dBFT)
    C. Loopchain Fault Tolerance(LFT)
    D. Delegated Proof of Stake

25. What is the document proposed as "must read" for bitcoin?
    A. The Bitcoin Manifesto
    B. The Bitcoin White Paper
    C. The Bitcoin Constitution
    D. Bitcoin and the Blockchain
26. Which bitcoin exchange in Japan was hacked in 2014?
    A. Tradehill
    B. Bit Tradde
    C. Bitstamp
    D. Mt.Gox

27. How many botcoins will ever be created?
    A. 210000
    B. 2100000
    C. 21000000
    D. Unlimited

28. You can send a bitcoin on Ethereum address:
    A. True
    B. False

29. The nodes which creates new blocks are called?
    A. Account holders
    B. Miners
    C. Verifiers
    D. Mitigators

30. The central server of Bitcoin is located at:
    A. Washington DC
    B. Japan
    C. Undisclosed Location
    D. No central server

31. What information does a wallet contain?
    A. Key pairs for each of your addresses
    B. Transactions done from/to your addresses
    C. Default key
    D. Reserve keys
    E. Version Number
    F. All of the above
    G. None of the above

Answers

Chapter 1: Blockchain Basics

1. **D** (Satoshi Nakamoto)

Explanation: Blockchain was invented by Satoshi Nakamoto.

2. **D** (Decentralized ledger distributed over p2p network)

Explanation: The blockchain is a technology which distributed decentralized ledger over p2p network.

3. **B** (Blockchain)

Explanation: The blockchain is decentralized ledger tracking digital assets on the p2p network.

4. **C** (Decentralized network)

Explanation: In Decentralized networks, controls are being distributed among the multiple nodes.

5. **B** (Distributed network)

Explanation: In Distributed network, controls are being distributed among all nodes.

6. **B** (Cryptocurrency)

Explanation: Bitcoin is an application of blockchain technology, in which Bitcoin is used as a cryptocurrency.

7. **C** (Block)

Explanation: The transactions associated to the user bitcoin's address are stored on a block of a Blockchain.

8. **B** (Proof of Work)

Explanation: The "Proof of work" algorithm is used in bitcoin application.

9. **C** (Toy Golden Unicorn)

Explanation: Bitcoin is equal to toy golden unicorn.

10. **B** (Smart Contract)

Explanation: The smart contract is used to define the computer program code that is capable of the facility, executing and enforcing the negotiation or the performance of an agreement by using blockchain technology.

11. **D** (Trustless)

Explanation: High security, High availability, Verifiability and auditability, Trustless are the benefits by using blockchain technology.

12. **C** (Feb 2014)

Explanation: NEO was launched in February 2014.

13. **A** (2)

Explanation: There are two functions of the blockchain database

- Read
- Write

14. **B** (4)

Explanation: There are four functions of the traditional blockchain

- Create
- Read
- Update
- Delete

15. **B** (Blockchain mining)

Explanation: Process of recording the pending transaction by adding a new block into the blockchain through mathematical puzzle (proof of work) is called blockchain mining.

16. D (All of above)

Explanation: Miner is referred to a computer or server which does all the required computation to validate the transactions & add new block into the blockchain. For this computation, miner is awarded.

17. D (All of above)

Explanation: Bitcoin, ethereum, and NEO are the application of blockchain.

18. A (2)

Explanation: There are two types of blockchain developer.

- Blockchain core developer
- Blockchain software developer

19. A (Initial Coin Offering)

Explanation: ICO stands for Initial Coin Offering.

20. B (3)

Explanation: There are three kinds of ethereum applications.

- Financial application
- Semi-financial application
- Nonfinancial application

21. A (Stellar's SDEX Exchange)

Explanation: Which is designed to find the rates between two digital assets and making it trade crypto is called stellar's SDEX exchange.

22. A (January 2009)

Explanation: Nakamoto implemented the bitcoin software as open source code and released it in January 2009.

23. B (July 2015)

Explanation: Ethereum was launched in July 2015.

1. B (Public and Private Key)

Explanation: Asymmetric encryption uses public and private keys to encrypt and decrypt data.

2. C (A key does not give to the public)

Explanation: It is a secret number that allows bitcoins to spent. Each an every Bitcoin wallet holds one or more private keys, which have saved in the wallet file.

3. D (A block reward)

Explanation: The incentive for dedicating computing resources to the network and continuously expending energy to verify transactions is the block reward and transaction fees.

4. D (Prevents double spending)

Explanation: It tries a different strategy for spending a prevents double with the same nonce. First A sends transaction A0 to B, and then it sends another transaction A0 to C.

5. A (A Decentralized Application)

Explanation: Decentralized applications (DAPP) are applications that run on a P2P network of computers rather than only one computer.

6. A (Mining)

Explanation: Asymmetric cryptography is a branch of cryptography where a secret key can divide into two parts, a public key, and a private key. While A passphrase is similar to a password because the password has generally referred to something used to authenticate or log into a system. A password generally refers to a secret used to protect an encryption key. When mining has not used in this type of scenario

7. D (All of the above)

Explanation: Digital currencies are the well-known type of digital token.

Utility tokens give a user to use a platform

The privacy-centric digital currency Monero (XMR) uses code that allows transaction amounts.

8. C (On an exchange)

Explanation: Many investors buy a cryptocurrency from an exchange. However, like any other online entity, the exchanges are vulnerable to hacking

9. C (Satoshi Nakamoto)

Explanation: The original inventor of Bitcoin is Satoshi Nakamoto.

10. D (Peer to Peer)

Explanation: Peer-to-Peer (P2P) represents the computers that participate in the network are peers to each other.

11. B (A computer on a Blockchain network)

Explanation: A node can be an active electronic device, including a computer, phone or even a printer, as long as it has connected to the internet and as such has an IP address.

12. D (Floppy Disk)

Explanation: Cryptocurrency wallets are specific to the cryptocurrency that has stored inside them.

13. B (Computers that validate and process Blockchain transactions)

Explanation: Miners tend to invest in compelling computing devices known as CPUs (central processing units) or GPUs (graphics processing units).

14. B (All of the above)

Explanation

- Cryptocurrency exchanges (online)
- Bitcoin ATMs (you put money inside and can load your bitcoin wallet)
- Bitcoin Voucher Cards (i.e., Austrian Post office, House of Nakamoto, Azteco London)
- Buy it personally from other people

15. C (A peer to peer network on a distributed ledger)

Explanation: The blockchain is a decentralized distributed ledger on a peer-to-peer network, which maintains a continuously growing number of transactions and data records.

16. A (A fork)

Explanation: In a hard fork, If one group of nodes continues to use the old software while the other nodes use the new software, a split can occur.

17. D (A paper wallet)

Explanation: Cold storage is an offline wallet delivered for storing bitcoins. The simple type of cold storage is a paper wallet.

18. A (The first block after each block having)

Explanation: The first block of a blockchain is a genesis block. The latest versions of Bitcoin number it as block 0, though very early versions counted it as block 1.

19. C (Gas)

Explanation: It can execute scripts using an international network of public nodes. Gas is an internal transaction pricing mechanism, is used to mitigate spam and allocate resources on the network.

20. B (A transaction and block verification protocols)

Explanation: It is also a mechanism for confirming the transactions and place a number of their coins on a block to confirm a transaction block.

21. A (A value in each block filled by miner)

Explanation: Nonce is an empty value in each block that is filled by the miner of that block.

Chapter 3: Blockchain Advanced

1. B. (Private Blockchain)

Explanation: Private blockchain is accessible to only those who get the permissions from the authorized parties, it may be an individual or an organization.

2. A. (Public Blockchain)

Explanation: Public blockchain is a permission less blockchain, anyone can easily access to them.

3. D. (All of the above)

Explanation: Only authorized nodes can read and write the ledger information.

4. C. (Miners)

Explanation: keep a few things in mind while setup your own blockchain that you have to take care of miners and setup your own miners.

5. E. (All of the above)

Explanation: We can setup our own blockchain by Ethereum, OpenChain, Multichain, Hyperledger fabric, and Bitcoin.

6. B. (Multichain)

Explanation: Multichain is an open source platform and founded by Mr. Gideon Greenspan.

7. D. (Hyperledger fabric)

Explanation: Private blockchain can be setup by Hyperledger fabric because it doesn't have the concept of Mining or Cryptocurrency.

8. A. (Hyperledger)

Explanation: Hyperledger is actually the project hosted by Linux foundation umbrella and fabric is one of the project hosted under the Hyperledger project.

9. B. (Store large data)

Explanation: Blockchain is distributive in nature, so it does not store large string of data. Therefore, blockchain is not useful in such case.

10. C. (Share common database)

Explanation: When organization need to share a common database across their employees, contractors, or third-parties, the permissioned blockchain can really fit into this situation.

11. B. (Defining the Goal)

Explanation: Blockchain building start with appropriate goal that it is beneficial for you.

12. D. (Integrate Upcoming Technologies)

Explanation: Blockchain solution can be integrated by emerging technologies to enhance its capability like Artificial Intelligence, Biometrics, Cloud, Cognitive services, Internet of Things, Machine Learning.

13. C. (Designing the Admin-User Interface)

Explanation: Designing the Admin-User Interface is separate step of building blockchain not the part of building APIs.

14. D. (All of the above)

Explanation: Each block consists of hash pointer to the previous block, Timestamp, List of transactions.

15. B. (More than one)

Explanation: Decentralized network has more than one parent node with many child nodes

16. D. (All of the above)

Explanation: All options are valid for decentralized network.

17. C. (Anyone requested for transaction)

Explanation: Blockchain processing begins with the person request for transaction in blockchain.

18. C. (Validation & Verification)

Explanation: These nodes validate the transaction and the user's status by using consensus mechanism.

19. A. (Creating a new block)

Explanation: When transaction has been verified by all the nodes of the network then transaction is combined with the existing transactions to create a new block of data for the ledger.

20. B. (Modified)

Explanation: Modified data is the most appropriate option.

21. C. (Transaction is Completed)

Explanation: The working of blockchain architecture completes with requested transaction become permanent part of the blockchain.

22. C. (Smart coding)

Explanation: Smart contract works smartly with smart programming code.

23. D. (Ethereum)

Explanation: Ethereum is the most preferred choice because it provides scalable processing capabilities.

24. C. (Distributed leger)

Explanation: Triggering an event occurs after the distributed ledger among all the nodes.

25. A. (Previous block)

Explanation: In blockchain, blocks are linked with previous block as the paper of the book.

Chapter 4: Blockchain Use-Case

1. **A** (It is a decentralized distributed database of immutable records)

Explanation: In blockchain technology, digital information is distributed among peers all over the world, this information is distributed, not stored at any single location, all records are public and easily verifiable, since it is being distributed among thousands of machines block chaining is nothing but a ledger.

2. **B** (Satoshi Nakamoto)

Explanation: Blockchain was invented by Satoshi Nakamoto in 2008 to serve as the public transaction ledger of the cryptocurrency bitcoin.

3. **A** (Vitalik Buterin)

Explanation: Vitalik is the creator of Ethereum. He first discovered blockchain and cryptocurrency technologies through Bitcoin in 2011.

4. **C** (SHA-256)

Explanation: SHA-256 is used in the creation of bitcoin addresses to improve security and privacy.

5. **A, C** (Block & Transactional records)

Explanation: Two types of records in blockchain database are block records and transactional records. Both these records can easily be accessed, and the best thing is, it is possible to integrate them with each other without following the complex algorithms.

6. **D** (All of above)

Explanation: Each block consists of cryptographic hash of previous block, timestamp and transaction data.

7. **A** (1)

Explanation: Each block references a previous block, also known as the parent block, in the "previous block hash" field, in the block header.

8. **F** (All of the above)

Explanation: Following are the consensus algorithm

- PBFT (Practical Byzantine Fault Tolerance)
- Proof-of-work
- Proof-of-stake
- Delegated proof-of-stake
- Proof-of-elapsed time

9. **C** (3)

Explanation: There are three types of Blockchains:

- Public
- Private
- Consortium

10. **E** (All of the above)

Explanation: Blockchain can be implemented of any sort of ledger.

11. **A** (Smart Contracts)

Explanation: A smart contract is a computer protocol intended to digitally facilitate, verify, or enforce the negotiation or performance of a contract. Smart contracts allow the performance of credible transactions without third parties. These transactions are trackable and irreversible.

12. **B** (Advanced Technology)

Explanation: We cannot use traditional technology and continue to digitize real estate transactions. Advance digitization of the process could make a considerable difference. Everybody has established a reliable solution for creating, enacting, verifying, storing and securing digital contracts.

13. **C** (Four)

Explanation: The system sends four copies of the contract, one for the seller, for the Purchaser, for the agent and for the Purchaser's bank.

14. **D** (Purchaser, Seller, Agent)

Explanation: The Purchaser, Seller, as well as the agent, each saves a copy of the contract, as well as a copy for the Purchaser's bank, and the Purchaser may now move into the property.

15. **A** (Three)

Explanation: Seller has signed the bill of sale, transfer the possession of the property and make the final payment.

16. **A** (Private master key)

Explanation: Digital identity is the common name given to an account's profile info, corresponding to the private master key that belongs to a user.

17. **B** (2-3%)

Explanation: A blockchain reduces the costs to 2-3% of the total amount and provides guaranteed, real-time transactions across borders.

18. **C** (New Customer)

Explanation: A customer loyalty program permits companies to attract new clients and hold clients with special discounts and deals.

19. **C** (SHA-256)

Explanation: SHA-256 is used in several different parts of the Bitcoin network:

- Mining uses SHA-256 as the Proof of work algorithm.
- SHA-256 is used in the creation of bitcoin addresses to improve security and privacy.

20. **B** (Hash Pointer)

Explanation: Hash pointer of each block links with the previous block in a blockchain. Hash stored in the hash pointer is the hash of the whole data of the previous block.

21. **A** (Spending a digital token multiple times)

Explanation: It's a condition when one digital token is spent multiple times because the token generally consists of a digital file that can easily be cloned.

22. **D** (All of the above)

Explanation: There are three types of ledgers; Centralized, Decentralized and Distributed.

23. **B** (Cross-border Payments)

Explanation: Ripple is used for cross-border payments.

24. **B** (Delegated Byzantine Fault Tolerance (dBFT))

Explanation: Delegated Byzantine Fault Tolerance (dBFT) is used as consensus algorithm in NEO.

25. **B** (The Bitcoin Whitepaper)

Explanation: Satoshi authors and releases a white paper titled Bitcoin: A Peer-to-Peer Electronic Cash System. This document is referred as must read document to understand the concept of block chaining.

26. **D** (Mt. Gox)

Explanation: Mt. Gox was a bitcoin exchange based in Shibuya, Tokyo, Japan. The company issued a press release on February 10, 2014, stating that the issue was due to transaction malleability: "A bug in the bitcoin software makes it possible for someone to use the bitcoin network to alter transaction details to make it seem like a sending of bitcoins to a bitcoin wallet did not occur when in fact it did occur.

27. **C** (21,000,000)

Explanation: 21 Million is the maximum cap which is not yet fully mined.

28. **B** (False)

Explanation: You cannot send bitcoin directly to an Ethereum address.

29. **B** (Miners)

Explanation: Miners are the creator of new blocks in a blockchain.

30. **D** (No Central Server)

Explanation: Blockchain technology is depends upon decentralized network & distributed database.

31. **F** (All of the above)

Explanation: Wallet contain Wallet.dat file containing:

- Keypairs for each of your addresses
- Transactions done from/to your addresses
- User preferences
- Default key
- Reserve keys
- Accounts
- A version number
- Key pool
- Info about current chain